# CIRCLES

# OF

# ANGELS

© 1999 HSA Publications 4 West 43rd Street, New York, NY 10036

HSA-UWC
4 West 43rd Street
New York, NY 10036

ISBN: 978-0-578-18059-5

© 1999 by Family Federation for World Peace and Unification

All rights reserved. No part of this book may be reproduced or
transmitted in any form or by any means, electronic or mechanical,
without permission in writing from the publisher, except by a reviewer
who may quote brief passages in a review.

*This book is dedicated to God, our loving parents, and the many mentors who assist our lives and lead us to our ever-expanding understanding of our Creator's original intention for the human family.*

# ONTENTS

A Prayer for the Reader . . . . . . . . . . . . . . . 1
Introduction . . . . . . . . . . . . . . . . . . . . . . 5

## PART ONE

Angel Bands . . . . . . . . . . . . . . . . . . . . . . . . . . . . . . . .
Organizing the Angels . . . . . . . . . . . . . . . . . . . . . . . . . .
My Own Band of Angels . . . . . . . . . . . . . . . . . . . . . . . 19
Who Are the Angels? . . . . . . . . . . . . . . . . . . . . . . . . . . 21
What Do the Angels Do? . . . . . . . . . . . . . . . . . . . . . . . 25

## PART TWO

Your Personal Circle of Angels . . . . . . . . . . . . . . . . . . . 29
Summoning the Angels . . . . . . . . . . . . . . . . . . . . . . . . 30
A Prayer to Summon Your Circle of Angels . . . . . . . . . . . 32
Gratitude . . . . . . . . . . . . . . . . . . . . . . . . . . . . . . . . . 35

Heavenly Guests ........................................... 37
Some Soul-Cleansing Ideas ............................ 39
A Prayer for Heart Cleansing ......................... 41
Healing in Forgiveness ................................... 43
A Prayer of Forgiveness .................................. 47
Healing Historic Hurts ................................... 49
A Prayer for the Healing of Historic Sins ....... 53
Responsibility and Service .............................. 55
Healing ........................................................... 59

## PART THREE

Stories of Angel Help—Unseen Protectors ...... 61
Waiting in the Wings ..................................... 65
My Faithful Guard ......................................... 67
Opening the Floodgates of Communication ... 69
Angels on the Job ........................................... 71
A Message to Be Shared ................................. 73

# Part Four

Epilouge........................................... 77
Angels In the Workplace .......................... 79
   An Accreditation Visit...................... 82
   Gratitude Inspires........................... 84
   Help for a Grieving Loved One ............. 86
   Embracing the World With Love ............ 87

Suggested Reading .............................. 89
About the Author ............................... 90

## *A PRAYER FOR THE READER*

*Lord,*
*Let this small book open*
*the doors of heaven for every reader.*
*Let it bring heaven and earth closer;*
*Let it enhance our quality of life;*
*and bring peaceful energy to our planet;*
*Let bands of angels multiply until*
*every soul on earth*
*is surrounded by and bathed in*
*The brilliant light of heavenly hosts.*
*Dear Lord,*
*We send our gratitude heavenward in praise*
*and earthward in love.*
*Amen*

*illions of spiritual creatures  
walk the earth unseen,  
Both when we walk  
and when we sleep;  
all these with ceaseless praise  
His works behold  
both day and night.*  
　—*John Milton*

# INTRODUCTION

Angels are making their presence known in unprecedented ways. At this time in history, spiritual energies, long unknown to most of us, are surfacing in the consciousness of humankind. Massive changes are occurring throughout the world. Like one generation giving birth to another, Mother Earth herself seems to be enduring chaotic labor pains, pushing mightily against old boundaries and limitations until life bursts forth into an age of transcendent spirituality.

There is also a universal acceleration of the healing of humankind. Humanity appears to be moving toward its true and original nature; there to find a home in the heavenly Father-Mother, God. Today we begin to sense as a reality

*eaven appears to be approaching earth in this century and with such acceleration that is quite different from all other times when a similar thing was happening....*

*What we are now experiencing is something so radical that I cannot point to any historical period during which the same thing happened. It is as if heaven and earth are on a collision course. What is hanging over our heads is a breakthrough of the unperceived world. The return of the angels could be one of the greatest surprises of the twentieth century.*

—H.C. Moolenburgh,
 *A Handbook on Angels*

that the global family is being prepared as a place where the spirit of God may truly dwell. So too the world of angels is making its presence known among us. Like midwives, angels are helping to move the process along—comforting, consoling, guiding, protecting, encouraging—usually without thanks or even recognition.

Now is the time for angels to be recognized and understood, even empowered. It is time for humankind to get in touch with the undercurrent of spiritual energy uniting everyone on earth and linking us to heaven.

Yes, the angels are undeniably among us. It is to our benefit to recognize their service in healing and protecting us. Angels are preparing for heaven to exist on earth and for the dwelling of God among us. Their work with us, however, can be much more powerful if we learn to call on them— invite them into our lives.

This little book about circles of angels is not only to inform and inspire; it is a manual on how to work with angel powers. It is for you, the readers, to know that you can invite your own circle of angels to surround and work with you. It is the angels' announcement that they are waiting to help you. It is for you to know their presence and their anticipation of your calling on them. Invisibly surrounding you, they know that this is the moment for humanity's spiritual birth. They eagerly long for your commission. Like many of us, they await the time when we will no longer "see through a glass darkly, but face to face." (I Corinthians 13:12). In turn, we will help the angels find their own fulfillment and joy in serving God's earthly family.

May this book open the angels' gift to you. It is a gift that will never end. Your circle of angels can be your enduring companion—bringing joy and goodness throughout your life. Call those who seek only goodness to surround you.

> "In the last days...I will pour out my spirit upon all flesh."—Acts 2:17

Here is their love to you.

PART ONE

# ANGEL BANDS

It began when I was sitting in my office looking at stacks of papers, each representing a project, a group of people, or an undeveloped idea. I felt overwhelmed, wondering how I could bring each of these tasks and projects to completion.

I pondered how I could delegate some of this work. To whom could I give these projects? I needed God's perspective. I asked how I might engage spiritual help.

Working through the stacks, I found myself humming a piece of a song remembered from childhood:

> Oh come, angel band!
> Come and around me stand.

An Angel band! What an interesting concept. I envisioned a band of angels surrounding me—ready to help. Yes, that was it—I would call on them for help. Was there not some understanding that their help was only a prayer away? My sense of feeling overwhelmed vanished as the angel band idea took shape.

I kept envisioning a circle of heavenly beings dancing around me. They were comforting and peaceful, and created a warm feeling. They were also energetic and vibrant. They were a special band of angels, united in heart and creating spiritual energy for healing, protection, and inspiration. I could sense the stirring of the air as they whirled around me.

When I browsed through new releases in bookstores, I was fascinated with the current interest in angels. It seems that we are finally becoming aware of spiritual help which was always available! Is God, with infinite love, sending greater angelic energy to earth, moving us toward a more spiritual age? Although I had always believed in angels, I began to feel a new excitement about the possibility of greater spiritual energy waiting to be released.

If greater spiritual power is available, perhaps I could tap into it—for example, visualizing bands of angels around those I prayed for might make my prayers more expansive, more comprehensive, and more powerful.

According to most definitions, angels are God's special servants, created to protect, guide, guard, help, heal and comfort us and to act as messengers.

Angels are believed to be practically innumerable. The Bible refers to their being called by the tens of thousands, and that myriads of heavenly hosts are being "poured out" upon the earth.

If they are awaiting a commission, how do I summon them? Thus began an exciting personal journey into a realm of learning how to engage spiritual help and companionship.

*ome let us join
our cheerful songs
with angels around
the throne;
Ten thousand are
their tongues,
But all their joys are one.*
  —Isaac Watts

*eep on loving each other
as brothers.
Do not forget
to entertain strangers
for by so doing some people have
entertained angels without
knowing it.*
  —Hebrews 13:1-2

## Organizing the Angels

"Everyone, no matter how humble he may
be, has angels to watch over him.
They are heavenly, pure, and splendid, and
yet they have been given us
to keep us company on our way...
They are at your side, helping your soul
as you strive to go ever higher in your union
in God and through Christ."
—Pope Pius 12th

Looking again at the many projects awaiting my attention, I decided to commission a band of angels as helpers. I first focused on all the particular things to be accomplished—many of these tasks depended on the cooperation of other people.

Before I could receive their cooperation, each of these people needed something.

- ❧ Some needed to be inspired.
- ❧ Some needed to be convinced.
- ❧ Some were waiting for doors to open up for them.
- ❧ Some needed to be prodded.
- ❧ Some were waiting for others to respond to them.
- ❧ Some had health, family or financial problems which needed attention.

Could I call a band of angels to help make each person's life flow more smoothly? If so, would the projects I was working on become easier to achieve? Why not?

I made a chart identifying each project by name, together with the people whose cooperation was required. Under each of those projects I listed the kinds of help needed. For example:

- ❧ One person's health problems were a deterrent to meeting important deadlines. She needed a healing angel band.

- Another's difficulty with relationships upset the harmony and flow of work. He needed angelic wisdom and harmony.
- Another person was not American. Sometimes cultural misunderstandings stood in the way of smooth decision-making. He and those with whom there were conflicts needed circles of understanding or mediating angels.
- Another person carried deep feelings of historic pain from racial discrimination, which surfaced in the form of resentment and required consideration at the most impossible times. She needed to be surrounded by healing, comfort and compassion for others.
- Another person was brilliant. When inspired, she produced efficiently and well. But she was not always inspired. She needed angels of encouragement and constancy.
- Still another person was conscientious in her leadership role, but quick to anger. Control issues stood in the way of two-way communication—often discouraging others

*ut to what angel has he ever said, 'Sit at my right hand, till I make my enemies a stool for thy feet?' Are they not all ministering spirits sent forth to serve for the sake of those who are to obtain salvation?*
   *—Hebrews 1:13-14*

on her team. She needed an angel band of nurture, comfort and love to heal her own past wounds.

As an over-achiever, I had taken on too much, and was feeling overwhelmed. There were the women's conferences we were setting up, speakers to engage, deadlines, finances to arrange, printing jobs, and so on. There were books I was trying to complete. There was the Fourth World Women's Conference in Beijing, China. I was responsible for a seminar my own women's organization was sponsoring there. There were many difficulties in making arrangements with a foreign government.

On a personal level I thought about my husband and grown children. Everyone had needs. The children were in college and often needed protection and guidance in making choices. There were financial needs to be met. My husband had his own career-related frustrations.

I decided that creating a circle of angels for each person and area of responsibility might make all our lives flow more harmoniously and free us to be more productive. I wrote down all the projects and people in my life—both personal and career-related. I listed the needs which the power of angel bands might meet to harmonize relationships and increase the flow of productivity. It was a spiritual organization chart.

Then I prayed over each item on my list, calling on God to send a circle of angels to surround each project and person.

I gave each circle of angels a name corresponding to the project. Under each name were listed very specific requests for help. In essence, each angel circle was commissioned with an earthly mission. Since that initial request, I send occasional prayers to thank them. I now feel like the director of a large service agency. On second thought, I not only feel like it, I am! Having circles of angels working on every project has become a way of life for me. It is a whole new way of thinking.

## My Own Band of Angels

While visiting New England I was waiting in a van while a friend picked up her children from school. Colored leaves danced above me in the wind. The sun was bright; the sky was blue. It was a wonderful time to enjoy nature, but my own mind was troubled by a difficult time I was having with someone. As I waited I felt a warm embrace in the air and sensed God's comforting smile. He seemed to be saying, "I've created an angel band for you." Suddenly I laughed. I had been creating circles of angels for everyone else, but I had not invited one specifically for myself. Yes, of course, I needed one too. "Thank you," I smiled back, and put my angel band to work—on me! It was so beautiful and real I wanted to cry. Basking in that warm embrace, I knew that such bands, or circles of angels, although invisible, were indeed real.

*ush my dear, lie still
and slumber
Holy angels guard your heart.
Heavenly blessings without
number
Gently falling on thy head.*
   —Isaac Watts, Divine Song,
      A Cradle Hymn

# Who Are the Angels?

"Around our pillows, golden ladders rise,
and up and down the skies,
with winged sandals shod, the angels come
and go, the messengers of God!"
—H.S. Stoddard, Hymn to the Beautiful

Angels are the spiritual part of God's creation. Created as the spiritual support system for God's family—humankind—they never experienced life in physical form as we know it. Many people think of loved ones who have passed on to eternal life, or the spiritual realm, as angels. They, too, are spiritual beings, and may come to help their loved ones on earth. However, they are distinguished here from the angels who were created by God for the specific purpose of serving

God's children—the human family. The angels can and do relate to our spiritual nature in ways of which we are often unaware.

According to some angelologists and theologians, those angels who center on the throne of God are available to fulfill the purpose of good only, and will not respond to selfish requests which could hurt others. Their purpose is to fulfill God's Will, to represent God's unconditional love for us, and to assist in anything which promotes the spiritual protection and growth of ourselves and those around us. In seeking angelic help, it is important to center ourselves with God first in order to protect ourselves from any influences that may be selfishly motivated and hurtful to us or others. Negative thoughts and motivations may draw in darker energies, which are helpful to no one. On a less personal level, angels help bring rebirth to the world, drawing and reshaping people ever closer to God's original intention. As angels protect more people from the forces of evil, they bring humanity closer and closer to God's own parental heart.

*ecause He is love in its essence, God appears before the angels...as a sun.*
*And from that sun, heat and light go forth; the heat being love and the light, wisdom.*
*And the angels' love and wisdom, comes not from themselves but from God.*
   *—Emanuel Swedenborg,*
   *Angelic Wisdom*

## WHAT DO THE ANGELS DO?

"For he will command his angels concerning you to guard you in all your ways; they will lift you up in their hands, so that you will not strike your foot against a stone."—Psalms 91:11-12

Angels, as servants, perform many duties. As they work with us, they grow and mature in their own wisdom and abilities. There are, for example:

| | |
|---|---|
| Guiding angels | bringing inspiration, truth, and wisdom. |
| Protecting angels | guarding, protecting and serving as |

| | |
|---|---|
| | a shield from the evils of the spiritual world and the dangers of the physical world. |
| Comforting angels | ministering to those in spiritual or physical pain, and to those who are grieving, struggling, depressed, or frustrated. |
| Angels of mercy | attending those who are suffering in poverty and pain. |
| Peace angels | visiting areas of conflict to inspire resolution, and bringing an atmosphere of harmony. |
| Angels of glory | glorifying God and carrying thoughts of praise to heaven from earth. |
| Angels of hope | bringing hope to the hopeless. |
| Angels of virtue | assisting in the development of character. |

| | |
|---|---|
| Angels of happiness | bringing joyful energy; helping us find happiness in the simple things of life. |
| Angels of encouragement | encouraging those who need a bit of gentle prodding to keep on growing. |
| Angels of love | nurturing the energy of love which is giving and unselfish. |
| Angels of grace | bringing the healing touch of grace and the ability to forgive oneself. |
| Angels of truth | guiding in the understanding of universal laws and truths of the universe. |
| Healing angels | mending a wounded or diseased body or spirit. |

PART TWO

# YOUR PERSONAL CIRCLE OF ANGELS

Some weeks after I first engaged the assistance of angel bands, I was counseling a friend who was struggling with a problem at work. I said, "Why don't you call an angel band to surround you and your co-workers?" I proceeded to tell her what I had done. Suddenly she said, "I see them coming! I see them forming a circle around me." Her response was all I needed to begin sharing the idea of circles of angels with other people.

## SUMMONING THE ANGELS

> "But if these beings guard you, they do so because they have been summoned by your prayers."—St. Ambrose

The angels are but a thought or prayer away. We are surrounded by thousands of invisible celestial beings who are ready, upon request, to serve our higher purpose.

A thought-form, or a prayer calling for angelic help brings them immediately to our side. They are always willing to receive our request, stay with us or be sent on a mission.

Since this is a time of cosmic change, the angelic world is becoming more visible in the lives of many people. These beings of light are helping to usher in a new age, and our awareness of their presence will only increase. Calling on a circle of angels to help in the healing of our planet, in the lives of those suffering around us, and in our own personal lives, is neither selfish nor a wasted use of a resource. Commissioning these heavenly hosts brings the energy of heaven's love to earth. As more of us facilitate angelic cooperation, higher energies are activated among us. We are already beginning to see changes happening which will help lead us toward a world of peace.

Why do the angels need to be summoned? It seems that, since they were created as God's messengers and servants, good angels will remain true to their purpose and not intervene in our lives without a request from us, an intercessor or God.

To call a circle of angels, it is wise to find a quiet place where you can meditate or pray. Let your heart be still. Contemplate those areas of your life which need improvement. Then simply ask God to give you a circle of angels to help carry out your work, improve your life, help you to love and serve others, and to grow in God's grace. Then thank God for the gift of an angel band.

## A Prayer to Summon Your Circle of Angels

*Oh Lord of Heaven, Father and Mother of all,*
*Thank you for your beautiful and intricate creation.*
*Please forgive me for not growing into my fullest potential.*
*Please forgive me when I allow myself to be drawn into darkness.*
*I humbly ask you today to send me a circle of angels to bring light and goodness into my life.*
*I pray for their energy to touch everything I do.*
*Let them bring a flow of harmonious joy into my life and the lives of those around me.*
*I ask the angels to enliven my mind to greater creativity; to purify my heart to greater compassion; to inspire me to greater generosity; and to fill me with greater love.*

*I thank you for the circle of angels you have sent to empower me with goodness.*
*I invite them to make their home with me. I thank my circle of angels for attending to my needs, for protecting and loving me and those around me.*
*I ask that with their help my life will be enlarged with greater goodness for the sake of all humanity and that the energy of one more circle of angels will add its power to the universe through me.*
*My heart is filled with gratitude.*
*Amen*

## Gratitude

"And all the angels stood 'round the throne
and 'round the elders
and the four living creatures, and they fell
on their faces before the throne and
worshiped God, saying Amen! Blessing and
glory and wisdom and thanksgiving
and honor and power and might be to our
God forever and ever! Amen."
—Revelation 7:11-12

None of us likes to work without recognition or reward. Gratitude is essential to the continued interest and engagement of your angel band. Indeed, gratitude is a healthy part of every relationship—whether with earthly or heavenly beings.

Since it is the mission of the angels to help us, they will do so at our request. A joyful angel band will also bring a joyful spirit around you. So thank them for their help, especially when you send them on a mission and when that mission is completed. Share the joy in a celebration of heart, song, prayer, and any other expression of gratitude. In relationship to God, angels as messengers can bring God's love to us and return praise and thanks to God.

## HEAVENLY GUESTS

As those heavenly bright lights sparkle around you; as they harmonize and love your world and make their home with you, your life will begin to sparkle. To maintain the sparkle and let it penetrate deep within you, it is beneficial for you to understand and address any dark shadows which may be lurking within and around you. Negative thoughts such as resentment, anger, depression, hatred, and fear, bring darkness to our souls.

We need a cleansing process much the same as we use when preparing for earthly guests. We clean the house, prepare food, and seek to make our guests comfortable. So it is with our new heavenly guests.

Both Jesus and John the Baptist spoke of repenting in preparation for the coming of the kingdom of heaven. To welcome our guests—our angels—from heaven it is wise to do a bit of personal soul-searching, general soul-cleansing, and amends-making in anticipation of their living and working among us. The suggestions in the following section will help you in your own cleansing process.

> "Angels of light, spread your bright wings and keep near to me at morn: nor in the starry eve, nor midnight deep, leave me forlorn. From all dark spirits of unholy power guide my weak heart. Circle around me in each perilous hour, and take my part. From all foreboding thoughts and dangerous fears, keep me secure; teach me to hope, and through the bitterest tears still to endure." —Unknown

## Some Soul-cleansing Ideas

At a time when you can be quiet and alone, take out three sheets of paper. Entitle the first, "Things I Have Done Which Have Hurt Others." Entitle the second, "People I Need to Forgive for How They Have Wronged Me." Entitle the third, "Historic Hurts."

Begin with page one. Letting your angels bring inspiration, make a lifetime list of every person you can remember to whom you have caused physical hurt or emotional pain. Beneath the names, list the things you've done. Start with your parents, then your friends, your teachers, your spouse and children, your boss or employees, and people with whom you have had business dealings. Think of times you've spoken badly about someone, times you've cheated people in money matters, times you may have abused anyone in any way—list everything. It is not easy to do, but you will find it enormously liberating. When you've finished the list, review it with a repentant heart. Call your angels and ask them to carry your repentance to God and the courts of heaven, even to those who have died. When possible, seek out the people you have hurt and offer your heartfelt repentance. Use wisdom in doing so, perhaps talking with a trusted counselor or friend, to be sure your amends will not harm you or anyone further. Amends should be made to others for wrong acts. You owe yourself amends for harmful feelings such as resentment. Where amends are necessary, make them, and for those who have passed on without your being able to make amends, ask the angels to carry your repentance to them.

Now let new joy fill your soul. Know that it is cleaner and clearer and that heaven's angelic hosts can make a home with you more easily.

## *A Prayer for Heart Cleansing*

*Dear God of unconditional love,
I am gratefully trusting in Your infinite and
unconditional love to which I open my life.
When I look at the hurts I have brought others,
I feel such sorrow, and emotions so deep I
almost fear to let them go.
I think of the times I have brought pain to
others—my family, my friends and those I've
held as enemies.
Admission of my own faults is so very difficult.
My God, I need your help to see my wrongs,
repent and make amends.
How often have I taken advantage of someone's
kindness or sought only my own interest, doing
damage to the fragile heart of another.
Forgive me, I beg, for my wrongs, both large
and small. Let my repentance open the doors of
communication between You and me.*

*Let it cleanse me of the negative energies
I have carried.
I seek forgiveness from those I have hurt.
I will make amends where possible and cleanse
myself of wrong actions.
I seek Your help that my future actions may
never again be hurtful.
I offer this prayer in gratitude for Your love and
forgiveness.
Amen*

## HEALING IN FORGIVENESS

Angels of God, My Guardian dear,
To whom God's love entrusts me here;
Ever this day be at my side,
To light and guard, to rule and guide.
—Traditional prayer

Move to your next sheet of paper: "People I Need to Forgive for What They've Done to Me." Ask the angels to help you with this part, for it may be even harder than repenting for your own wrong deeds. Let your mind search for the hurts in your life—jot down names and incidents as they come to your consciousness. Search your life diligently.

When your list is complete, contemplate each name or incident carefully, searching out the points where your heart has set up barriers and defenses. Begin your cleansing process with a short prayer of forgiveness for each entry.

The forgiveness process is an ongoing one. You continuously meet people and find new opportunities to serve, comfort, love, and forgive those who may have harmed you. You can start with a conscious decision to dismiss your resentments whenever you are aware that they occupy your thoughts. Send them away with one of your strongest angels!

Furthermore—send your angels to those who have passed on to the next world, that both your heart and theirs may be healed of those pains which block forgiveness. If appropriate, repent for the role you played in these hurtful relationships. It is possible that your resentment toward them can keep them from being able to go forward freely in the next life. This is especially true with your parents, grandparents, and relatives.

This exercise, although difficult, will not only prepare you to attract angels of a higher vibration; it will increase your health and radiance. Conversely, harboring negative feelings and thoughts that are burned deep in your soul has a powerful capacity to attract similar energy. This exercise of identifying such feelings and freeing yourself will have great benefits.

## *A Prayer of Forgiveness*

*Oh God of unlimited love and forgiveness;*
*Father and Mother of Mercy.*
*As I contemplate the times I've been hurt,*
*I see the heavy burden of resentment*
*and pain I've carried.*
*I want to be free—free to let my spirit fly*
*to Your pristine love.*
*I can no longer bear these dark thoughts*
*which bar me from your parental warmth*
*and light.*
*Now I ask Your assistance in forgiving those*
*who have wronged me.*
*I have suffered at the hand of others,*
*but I only hurt myself by continuing to carry*
*that suffering with me.*
*Grant me courage to forgive.*
*Grant me courage to let others know*
*I've forgiven them*
*directly or in the way I relate to them.*

*One by one, I forgive each person who has been
the source of my suffering.
Thank you, for helping me to do this.
Thank you for the new space
that has been created in my heart.
Thank you, for letting me fly!
Amen*

## HEALING HISTORIC HURTS

"Angels are powerful thought forms that help to hold the world together.
They are the thoughts of synthesis, connection, and repair.
To call on the angels is to move our attention to a higher, more creative direction, to invoke the structures of a more enlightened world view."
　—Marianne Williamson, Illuminata

Now move to the third topic: "Historic Hurts." Visualize your life as part of a larger whole, your family, ancestors, descendants, city, nation and the world—present and past. Visualize everything that is in your environment with which you have a connection. Let your mind search for unresolved resentments and pain.

For example, does your family history suggest that there are skeletons in closets which may come back to haunt you? The Bible mentions (Exodus 20:5-6) that the sins of the fathers are passed to the children for several generations. Did your ancestors hold slaves, take advantage of others, fight in wars? While many have fought for noble causes, regardless of the weight of justice in the conflict, everyone involved in wars resulting in deaths might well incur burdens of resentment from those affected by the conflicts. Are there stories of less than noble deeds performed by your ancestors or family? Does your country bear responsibility for hurting other races or nationalities either within or outside its borders? List whatever comes to your mind on this third sheet of paper.

To correct these problems you might seek someone who

represents the hurt ones and do a "random act of kindness." In some cultures, giving money to beggars on the street is viewed as a way to make amends for the sins of ancestors.

In offering money or service, you are participating not only in your personal cleansing, but in planetary healing. On a personal level, you are creating a larger and larger sphere of influence for your circle of angels—from deep within your soul to the edges of our planet and into the universe.

## *A Prayer for the Healing of Historic Sins*

*Dear Heavenly Parent,*
*I have reflected on, and repented for the sins of my father's and my lineage, and those with whom I have a connection.*
*I repent for:*

- *The pain they may have unwillingly inflicted.*
- *The wars they fought.*
- *The judgement they inflicted on others in a less enlightened time.*
- *The hurt to brothers and sisters of other races and cultures of our global family.*
- *The times others were abused in an effort to gain power and material wealth.*

∽   *The times women and children
    suffered abuse.*

*My Heavenly Parent, in their stead, I repent for
the sins of the past, asking You to forgive my
ancestors, my nation, and my people.
Thank you for the cleansing and liberation of
all historic wrongs in my lineage.
Amen*

## RESPONSIBILITY AND SERVICE

It is a universal law that giving produces receiving. In calling on a willing and helpful angel band, you are receiving heavenly help, joy, and inspiration. Their work and constancy with you will be much enhanced by your own heart of compassion and service.

The exercise of good will is contagious. Not only will your angels be pleased and bring you more and more good energy, but the people around you will also respond.

As love, compassion, and service become a way of life, you will find that good energy follows you everywhere you go. Certainly all of us know people who always seem to bring light into the atmosphere.

What is service? What could you do? Let me list a few ideas:

There is service of the heart, which we might call compassion. It is a practice of love—of smiling when someone needs encouragement, of mentioning someone's good points when others see only the bad. It is listening to someone who needs to be heard or understood. It is projecting warmth and positive energy which enables others to have the security and confidence to grow. It is really your own heart reaching out to another heart.

There is service of a helping hand—of giving a hand in time of need. A simple offering to help carry packages, give a lift, or relieve a burdened mother of her child for a period of time may seem so small, but simple acts can make a great impact. Developing a lifestyle which includes such acts on a regular basis will make a loving and serving attitude a natural part of your life, and give you a magnetic energy which will bring back to you love and service in turn. Working as a service project volunteer is another way of reaching out, returning to you great joy and reward. In our era of attention-seeking, self-interest, and self-protectiveness, we need to rediscover the joy of selflessness and service.

There is service from the pocket. It is a universal law that generosity brings its own returns. To learn the joy of giving and the expansion of heart required is an important part of our spiritual growth. Money becomes a vehicle not only for our own enjoyment, but also to bring others joy. When you have it, it is one of the easiest ways to serve or give.

# Healing

Do angels heal? Recently I heard an interesting story. An elderly man was extremely ill. His kidneys were failing, making him dependent on dialysis. In desperation he visited a psychic healer and was told that his illness was related to the fact that in his youth, he had worked in his country's World War II program testing the effects of chemical warfare on humans. Those who died from such testing carried deep resentment to their grave. This negative energy was surrounding him and affecting his health. The healer prayed for angels to cleanse his bloodstream and carry positive light energy throughout his body. This man's health took a miraculous turn for the better and within weeks he had begun to gain weight and walk again. I found this an interesting revelation on how angels help in the healing process. Angels always bring healing energy. Their presence, not only around our bodies but also within them, can bring about healing and cleansing. Sending the angels on healing missions is of equal help to body and soul. If you are having a health problem, the cleansing of your mind and drawing of angel energies can be a source of your own healing.

> "I, John, am he who heard and saw these
> things. And when I heard and saw them,
> I fell down to worship at the feet of the
> angel who showed them to me;
> but he said to me, 'you must not do that!
> I am a fellow servant with you and
> your brethren the prophets, and with those
> who keep the words of this book.
> Worship God!' "
> —Revelation 22:8-9

PART THREE

## STORIES OF ANGEL HELP— UNSEEN PROTECTORS

"Lord, send your angels to surround
me...Lord, don't let them be
transparent today, for the guards must not
see me!"
The guards passed by Corrie Ten Boom
when the prisoners were searched.
—Corrie Ten Boom, The Hiding Place

Shannon was on her way home from a visit to the doctor in which she had been told she would need surgery. Shannon was anxious and when she passed a large open church, she decided to enter and pray.

It was 3:30 on a sunny California afternoon. Shannon entered a pew, and kneeling, she began to pour out her heart to God. She became aware of the presence of another person beside her. Someone had entered the church. "This is odd," she thought, "In a big empty church, why would this man kneel beside me?" Suddenly the large man grabbed her, covered her mouth, and pinned down her arm. Shannon realized his intent as she tried to wrestle with him. "God, I need help," she prayed. Looking up to the right side she saw glitter-like flecks of gold in the air. She felt the presence of angels. Suddenly the attacker looked up, horrified, released Shannon and ran out of the church. Obviously, whatever he saw was powerful enough to frighten him. Shannon believes that those glittering flecks were a battalion of angels protecting her and that her attacker also saw them.

Later that week Shannon received three letters—all dated on that same February, 1980 date. Her friends stated that she had been on their minds that day. One said that he had awakened at exactly 3:30 p.m. from a nap and knew he had to pray for her.

How often have our unseen friends protected us from harm? Certainly there are many similar stories of angels working for our protection.

## Waiting in the Wings

After having written most of this manuscript, I shared it with a friend who was visiting from Texas. A heavy thunderstorm delayed her return to where she was staying, requiring her to leave my home quite late.

Several days later, she was back in Texas when I received a call from her. "Nora," she said, "Angel bands are wonderful—they work! What can I do to help you get the book published?" She went on to tell this story: While she was driving back to where she was staying, it was rainy and dark and she came across several accidents. Thinking about the manuscript she had just read, she decided to call a circle of angels for protection. Her thoughts continued to dwell on angel bands and she decided that, since she traveled a lot, she would call a circle of angels to protect her husband and each of her children. Upon her return to Texas the following day, her daughter said "Mommy, while you were gone, I heard you saying my name, but your voice was coming from inside of me. I knew you weren't here, but it made me feel so comfortable."

My friend's husband had been searching for the "right" job for two years. Both of them were frustrated about his not finding something to fit his interests. Two days after she had sent him a circle of angels, he received two job offers in his field of interest.

## MY FAITHFUL GUARD

On a visit to Denver, Colorado to give a seminar on Woman's Spirituality, I spent several nights at a friend's house. We had worked together at the NGO Forum in Beijing, China, and had, after many years, brought each other up to date on our spiritual progress and interests. Marlene knew I was aware of the seemingly cosmic spiritual changes that were taking place. She too had opened her mind and heart to healing energies and spirituality.

When I arrived at her house, Marlene exclaimed, "Nora, the angel Gabriel has been waiting here for you for two days. He's sitting in front of the guest room door." Since I do not "see" angels myself I was a bit surprised and was not quite sure what I should do with this information. I certainly felt protected during my stay.

Marlene, who has a stronger spiritual intuition than I, kept remarking that the house was full of angels during the visit. It is incidents like these that remind me to thank these heavenly companions for their protection and love.

# Opening the Floodgates of Communication

"The farther we go along the path of God,
the more angels we shall encounter."
—H.C. Moolenburg,
 A Handbook on Angels

On another occasion, I was in Madison, Wisconsin, giving a speech on Women's Spirituality and Healing. As I began my presentation there was the usual polite quietness. Some people were paying attention, but others looked preoccupied. It seemed a difficult audience to engage. But there was a point where the audience suddenly became animated.

I felt energized and the words began to flow. I could see that people were connecting to what I was saying. I remember thinking, "What did I say that made them suddenly come alive?"

After the speech was over, a young woman came up to me and said, "I want to tell you what happened during your speech. All of a sudden the room was filled with bright lights, and you became so beautiful." It looks like my angel band decided to give me a hand—especially on the "beautiful" part!

If we can realize how valuable these celestial beings are in our relationships with people, the flow of communication can be enhanced tremendously. After all, they are messengers! Communication is their business.

## ANGELS ON THE JOB

Within the last year, I presented an important proposal for consideration by a certain very distinguished committee. It was a decision which would have a great impact on the organization I represented. I also knew that the result of a negative decision would limit the work of the organization worldwide. Once again I called on not only my own circle of angels, but a whole battalion of them. I wondered how to best engage their assistance. So I made a plan, deciding to send a circle to all members of the committee ahead of time to help them understand the issues and prevent misunderstanding. On the day of the decision-making meeting, I asked tens of thousands of angels to permeate the room, and carry away any confusion or negative emotions.

The decision was made unanimously in favor of our organization. Some of my friends said, "While your organization was being discussed, the whole atmosphere seemed to be charged with spiritual energy."

Did it work? All I can say is, the results speak for themselves.

> "At the round earth's imagin'd corners,
> blow your trumpets, angels,
> and arise, arise from death,
> your numberless
> infinities of souls."
> —John Donne

## A Message to be Shared

"When at night I go to sleep,
Fourteen angels watch do keep."
From the opera, Hansel and Gretel

After writing this manuscript, I put it aside for a while. Then the news of Princess Diana's death shocked the world. For some reason, I felt drawn to pull out the manuscript and read it again, perhaps for my own consolation.

I felt a certain amount of vulnerability. No matter how much protection wealth or position can buy, one is never assured of the absolute protection of our physical life. As I pondered this thought, I realized that in the end, we have far greater peace of mind with a shield of protection provided by a circle of angels than with earthly bodyguards. Whenever I travel, whether by car, plane or train, I feel more secure when I call on my angels to encircle the vehicle in which I am traveling. Wherever my husband or children drive, I ask a circle of angels to protect them.

> And I heard a loud voice from the throne saying,
> "Behold, the dwelling of God is with men.
> He will dwell with them
> and they will be his people and God
> Himself will be with them…."
> —Revelation 21:3

Life is so resilient, yet so fragile. No matter how careful we are, there are always those who are not. How quickly life can be snuffed out or hurt by carelessness, either our own or others. There are always potential disasters. Rather than living in fear of the possible danger lurking around every corner,

I believe we may live in the glorious confidence and peace that is enhanced by deliberately and consciously surrounding ourselves with celestial friends. As more of us share this view, the more God's energy will be drawn to this earth.

Although one has only to notice medieval art to realize that circles of angels have been known throughout history, today heaven is opening up to us in a more powerful way. As a new era of spirituality, resplendent and warm with God's maternal love, makes itself known to us, our response need not be a mere passive one. From sweet cherubs to a powerful army of spiritual warriors, bands of angels wait at attention ready to serve. During this time when negative forces that cause pain, suffering, and self-absorption are being confronted and given opportunity for transition to original goodness, action is necessary. The separation of heaven's and earth's spiritual forces is narrowing as increasing numbers of us enhance our lives with the beautiful and joyful participation of Circles of Angels. In reading this book, my prayer is that you will consciously increase the angel power around you and share it with others.

As I write these final words, I look out my window to the rainy street below. Someone is walking by with an umbrella featuring an angel in every panel. Looking down on it, I see a circle of angels. I smile. Confirmation comes from the oddest places!

## *A Closing Prayer*

*Lord,*
*Let this small book open*
*The doors of heaven for every reader.*
*Let it bring heaven and earth closer.*
*Let it enhance our quality of life.*
*Let it bring peaceful energy to our planet.*
*Let bands of angels multiply until*
*Every soul on earth is surrounded by*
*And bathed in*
*the brilliant light of heavenly hosts.*
*Dear Lord,*
*We send our grateful praise*
*To heaven and commit*
*Our service to earth.*
*Amen*

# Epilogue

In the fifteen years since Circles of Angels was first published, many readers have expressed appreciation in knowing that they are able to invite angels into their lives. They have flourished in the enrichment that the presence of angels has brought to them.

My own life, I believe, has been much enhanced by surrounding myself and bathing my environment in the light, energy and assistance of angels. In responding to the numerous requests from readers for the book to be reprinted, I have added an update on my continued engagement of these heavenly helpers. The following stories provide insight into the everyday benefits of the companionship and assistance of angels.

"Angels descending, bringing from above, echoes of mercy, whispers of love." — Fanny J. Crosby, *Blessed Assurance*

# A Prayer of Gratitude

Dearest Father Mother God,
You have given us these beautiful,
loving heavenly hosts as your emissaries.
You have sent them to guide our path, to smooth our way
and to heal our hurts.
You have asked us to share them with others.
As healing angels reach out to those in pain
and as loving angels harmonize relationships
among people and nations,
your presence and the power of your love is increased in our lives.

Our Father Mother God,
We thank you and your heavenly messengers for the energy
that will sustain us as you embrace our world.
In gratitude for what has been accomplished
and for what will continue to be accomplished,
We thank all of heaven
and ask that your messengers will continue to bring forth love
into every corner of your creation.

---

EPILOGUE

## Angels in the Workplace

For most people the place of work is where we spend the greatest amount of time and intentional focus. We may be less inclined to call on the energy and support of angels to enhance the workplace. In this chapter, I would like to share some personal experiences with surrounding and infusing my own workplace with the greater momentum brought by angels.

Currently I am serving as a high school administrator in a private school, dealing with faculty, staff, students and parents — and noting their needs and situations. There are many opportunities for angels to bring joy and harmony into every situation.

This is how I have incorporated a "heavenly staff". In the process of reviewing lists of students, I ask for a circle of angels to surround and support each student and his or her family. The angels are given instructions to take away any interference that would negatively influence the students' school experience. Whenever problems such as academic difficulties, illnesses, emotional traumas, home or family issues occur during the school year, I ask the assigned angels to teach, heal, love, comfort, and remove those obstacles.

The need for disciplinary measures seems to be reduced by the presence and assistance of these circles of angels. Not only are angels commissioned to help each student; a circle is commissioned for staff, faculty members, special committees, trustees and recruitment efforts. I believe that the climate and culture of the school flows more smoothly and is much enhanced by angel energy. As always, it is a matter of faith, and usually one can only intuit the gift of the angels.

There are many issues confronting a highly diverse, international group of high school teens. A circle of angels can be a most valuable resource in assisting youth who are dealing with rejection, social pressure, bullying and distractions such as interest in the opposite sex and the use and/or misuse of technology. Many areas, whether hidden or open, require attention. Most significantly, everyone needs and desires to be loved. Would not the invisible presence of a warm, loving circle of angles make a difference in these young lives? There is harmony in places where angels abide.

Occasionally I become aware that a student started the school year late and thus fell outside the angel assignment radar. On one occasion where there were difficulties surrounding a particular student, I realized that this young man came later in the school year and had not been assigned an angel support team!

# An Accreditation Visit

An accreditation visit by a team of professional educators is no small event in the life of a school. Such a team, which consists of seven or more educators, evaluates the operation of a school and makes recommendations to an accrediting agency.

For our scheduled visit we made every effort to welcome the visiting team openly and have both faculty and students reach out to them to share the culture of our school.

On the second day of such a visit, one of our faculty members took me aside and said: "Nora, I had the same dream two nights in a row. In the dream I was given a pair of 3-D glasses and told to wear them. When I put them on I could see angels filling the corridors of the school. As the visiting team entered and walked down the corridor, the angels were greeting them all along the way. There was such a welcoming atmosphere. I think this dream was meant to be shared with you."

The message was that the angels helping our school wanted to make their presence known! The angels were summoned in the faith that they are bringing their energy to the projects to which they have been assigned. This confirmation was an added blessing and encouraged me to keep assigning and thanking them.

## Gratitude Inspires

It is easy to forget about specific tasks that have been assigned to our heavenly assistants, especially if the tasks are distant from our immediate life. One way I have found to keep in touch with them is by incorporating gratitude and recognition into my regular exercise program.

While doing arm and upper body exercises, I can feel energy being stirred up! I also pray, that energy will flow to my wonderful spiritual troops. While holding hand weights and moving my arms in circular inward movements, I call and pull in all the angels who have missions. At this time I thank them for their work and give them instructions. Then, reversing the arm exercises to outward circles, I send them to continue their work. I believe that the angels who have been commissioned will do what is asked, and if they feel appreciated and inspired will expend more energy through give and take with us! They give me energy! I, in turn, give them energy, and life moves forward with added impetus.

I would like to encourage the reader to be creative about commissioning a spiritual team to get involved in the physical world. See if you can feel a difference.

Lord,
Thank you for allowing each of us
to be a conduit for your love.

"Thy kingdom come.
Thy will be done on earth, as it is in heaven. . . ."

Matthew 6: 10 (KJV)
From the Lord's prayer

# Help for a Grieving Loved One

A woman who recently lost her husband told me that he had come to her after he had passed away and told her to surround herself with angels. He added that there are angels who help those who are grieving after the departure of a loved one. He also told her that there are angels everywhere ready to assist whenever we ask. I asked her if I could share this with the readers of this book.

What a comfort to know this. Hopefully, this knowledge will help many who are grieving. This is an example of the fact that angels are interested in our concerns, and that there are angels who specialize in helping people on earth with every kind of problem.

# Embracing the World with Love

It makes sense to me that when people are engaging and multiplying beneficial spiritual energy, the world will be a safer, more comfortable place for everyone.

Do not be hesitant to enlarge your circles. Ever-increasing circles of angels who are working on larger and larger "missions" may impact countries and governments, bring peace, healing and love in greater circles than we can even imagine.

By sending these good "vibes" around the world, we are a part of worldwide efforts to help usher in the long awaited peace that God so desperately desires.

I am reminded of Jesus' statement to Peter:

"And I will give you the keys of the kingdom of heaven, and whatsoever you bind on earth will be bound in heaven, and whatsoever you loose on earth will be loosed in heaven". Matthew 18:18.

The horizontal pathways evolving from technological innovations have created greater potential for world unity. Emails, Twitter, Facebook and Smart Phones are communications on a horizontal level. Such communication is only as good as the thoughts and ideas of the communicators. Our virtual world of connectivity will form a "cloud of goodness" around our world.

With more input of spiritual knowledge, energy and God's wisdom, world unity can take place on higher and higher levels of consciousness. Eventually we may see our world welcome the Kingdom of Heaven on Earth. We pray for this.

# SUGGESTED READING

Daniel, Alma, Wyllie, Timothy, Ramer, Andrew, and Posnakoff, A. Ask Your Angels, Ballantine Books, 1992.

Martin-Kuri, K., A Message for the Millenium (Currently out-of-print).

Moolenburgh, H.C., Marix-Evans, Amina (translator) A Handbook of Angels, Inland Book Co., 1989.

Moon, Sun Myung, Exposition of the Divine Principle, HSA-UWC, 1996.

Swedenberg, Emannuel, and Wunsch, William F., Angelic Wisdom About Divine Providence, Swedenborg Foundation, 1996.

Ten Boom, Corrie, Sherrill, John L. and Elizabeth, (Contributors) The Hiding Place, Fleming H Revell Co., 1996.

Williamson, Marianne, Illuminata: A Return to Prayer, Riverhead Books, 1995.

## About the Author

Nora M. Spurgin, MSW, is a psychotherapist who has always held a special interest in the empowerment and healing she believes is available to us through spiritual sources centered upon God.

In A Circle of Angels, she shares her thoughts and personal experiences in tapping the spiritual energy provided by angels.

Ms. Spurgin is also a public speaker and author and editor of numerous books and journals. She recently wrote Insights into the Afterlife, a book of questions and answers on life after death. In it she assures those who fear death and comforts those who are grieving the loss of a loved one. She helps us all prepare for the inevitable journey ahead.